About South East
Wales

Published by Graffeg
First published 2007
Copyright © Graffeg 2007
ISBN 978 1 905582 07 5

Graffeg, Radnor Court, 256 Cowbridge
Road East, Cardiff CF5 1GZ Wales UK.
Tel: +44(0)29 2037 7312
sales@graffeg.com www.graffeg.com
Graffeg are hereby identified as the
authors of this work in accordance
with section 77 of the Copyrights,
Designs and Patents Act 1988.

Distributed by the Welsh Books
Council www.cllc.org.uk
castellbrychan@cllc.org.uk

A CIP Catalogue record for this book
is available from the British Library.

Designed and produced by
Peter Gill & Associates
sales@petergill.com
www.petergill.com

Map base information reproduced
by permission of Ordnance Survey
on behalf of HMSO
© Crown Copyright.
All rights reserved. Ordnance Survey
Licence number 100020518

About South East Wales
Written by David Williams,
foreword by Siân Lloyd

The publishers are also grateful to
the Welsh Books Council for their
financial support and marketing
advice. www.gwales.com

Every effort has been made to
ensure that the information in this
book is current and it is given in good
faith at the time of publication. Please
be aware that circumstances can
change and be sure to check details
before making travel plans.

Front cover image: National Assembly
for Wales, Cardiff Bay.

About South East
Wales

Foreword

"Whether you live here or are visiting for the first time, I hope that this book will inspire you to explore Wales's many cultural and historical treasures, leading you to new and exciting experiences. It is intended to be a source book of ideas for things to do."

Wales is a remarkable part of the world where, over many centuries, people have created a rich and fascinating heritage. From battle-worn castles to settled towns and villages, from mines and quarries to elegant historic houses, there are tremendous places to visit.

Museums draw upon wonderful original material to tell our story. Many towns have local-history museums. The National Museum Wales, an impressive group of museums and galleries, illuminates our collective past through informative and innovative displays.

Our enthusiasm for culture, especially music and literature, is famous. Wales produces stars of concert hall, opera, stage, screen and rock arena – along with gifted writers and poets. There is strength in depth, from keen amateur activity in local halls and eisteddfodau to the thriving professional sphere. Major festivals, and smaller events, accommodate every cultural and artistic activity: music, literature, theatre, dance, the visual arts and others.

Wales asserts its cultural individuality in an increasingly interconnected and globalised world. The long history of the Welsh people has evolved into a forward-looking modern identity, based on respect for the past. As someone who works in both England and Wales, and travels widely, I enjoy sharing this distinctive sense of identity with people I meet.

I am fluently bilingual in Welsh and English and thank my parents for sending me to a Welsh school. The opportunities I received there – especially in public speaking, drama and music – set me on course to become a broadcaster.

The Welsh language, spoken by around half a million people, supports a wonderful literature and a thriving culture. English and Welsh enjoy official status together and many other languages are heard too, especially in the multicultural cities of Cardiff, Swansea and Newport.

Whether you live here or are visiting for the first time, I hope that this book will inspire you to explore Wales's many cultural and historic treasures. It is intended to be a source book of ideas for things to do. So, please enjoy the evocative photographs and learn interesting things but, above all, be sure to get out and about to experience the wonders of Wales for yourself.

Siân Lloyd

Wales Millennium Centre. This arts centre is unmistakely Welsh and internationally outstanding. What you see in and around it has been inspired by Welsh landscapes, people and Welsh tradition.

Introduction

This book celebrates the historical and cultural attractions that make south-east Wales such a special place. We hope that it will lead you to enjoyable discoveries and a deeper appreciation of this ancient and profoundly fascinating region and its people.

Located on the western side of the UK, Wales is bounded by the sea on three sides and shares a border with England to the east. Almost a quarter of its area enjoys special environmental designation.

Our three national parks – Snowdonia, the Brecon Beacons and the Pembrokeshire Coast – contain landscapes and habitats of international importance. Other regions throughout Wales are designated Areas of Outstanding Natural Beauty and there are more than 1,000 Sites of Special Scientific Interest.

But it is the way in which people have left their mark – on the landscape, in towns and cities, and on the world – that gives Wales its unique character. It is a place where a sense of history, and the achievements of the past, are valued by an advanced modern nation.

Wales is part of the United Kingdom and therefore is not fully a nation state. But its people certainly see themselves as a distinct nation. The Welsh language reinforces this identity, yet many people who do not speak it are also quick to assert their Welshness. The devolution of significant powers from Parliament in London to the National Assembly for Wales in Cardiff has given us one of the world's newest democratic institutions and greater autonomy.

Evidence of how people lived and worked over the centuries is preserved at our many ancient monuments, castles, historic houses and industrial locations. Wales has two UNESCO World Heritage Sites: the great medieval castles and town walls of north-west Wales and the industrial landscape of Blaenavon in the south-east.

Many places are in the care of either the National Trust or CADW, the Welsh Assembly Government's historic environment division. Museums and galleries, including the National Museum Wales, tell of our remarkable past.

The Welsh are seen as musically and lyrically gifted people. Ability in the areas is celebrated at local events and major festivals. The vigorous cultural life reflects the varied origins of the people (especially in the cities) and their typically open-minded gregariousness.

This book celebrates some of the historical and cultural attractions that make south-east Wales such a special place. We hope that it will lead you to enjoyable discoveries and a deeper appreciation of this ancient and profoundly fascinating region and its people.

David Williams

Above: **National Eisteddfod.**
Held at the beginning of August, the National Eisteddfod moves to a different part of Wales each year.

About this book

The aim of this book is to give you a taste of some of the main cultural and historical attractions of south-east Wales. It is one of a series of four regional pocket guides that cover, between them, the whole of Wales.

You will find information on many locations to visit and events to enjoy: castles, historic houses, industrial-heritage sites, museums, galleries, large festivals and local gatherings.

Each entry provides guidance on how to get there. Maps show the towns and villages mentioned, and the main roads. Contact information and website addresses will enable you to find current event programmes, opening times and any admission charges, and to plan your visit in detail.

We list the best-known attractions but, of course, Wales has such a rich heritage that there are many more places to explore. The main tourism websites – and those of organisations including CADW and the National Trust – are included here.

We also provide details of Tourism Information Centres, places to stay and eat, advice on south-east Wales's public transport system and an introduction to the Welsh language. The book concludes with an index of places, attractions, festivals and events.

We hope you enjoy browsing in search of interesting places to visit and things to do.

South East Wales
Wales's cosmopolitan capital city of Cardiff is within easy reach of relaxing countryside.

Above left: **Caerphilly Castle.** Proudly standing on a 30 acre site, Caerphilly Castle is one of the largest fortresses in Europe. Above right: **Cardiff Bay**. As Europe's largest waterfront development, Cardiff Bay has a wealth of leisure activities available on and off the water.

Contents

Welcome to South East Wales, where cosmopolitan style meets traditional values. The formerly industrial Valleys are known the world over for their culture and heritage. The gentle Vale of Glamorgan is a region of quaint villages and historic towns. Cardiff, the capital city of Wales, oozes style and a cutting-edge dynamism that amazes visitors. The peace and tranquillity of the Wye Valley and the Vale of Usk are a far cry from the sounds of border warfare that echoed here for centuries.

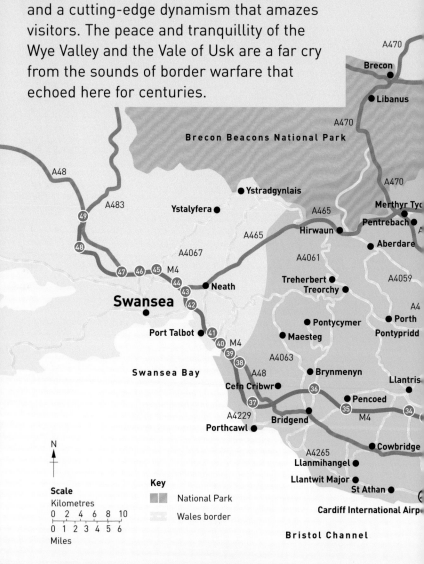

A470

● **Brecon**

● **Libanus**

A470

Brecon Beacons National Park

A48

A483

● **Ystradgynlais**

Ystalyfera ●

A465

Merthyr Tyc

Pentrebach ●

A465

Hirwaun ●

● **Aberdare**

A4067

A4061

A4059

Treherbert ●
Treorchy ●

A4

49

48

M4

47 46 45

44

● **Neath**

● **Porth**

Pontypridd

Swansea ●

43

42

● Pontycymer

Port Talbot ● 41

40

M4

39

● Maesteg

A4063

● **Brynmenyn**

Llantris

38

A48

Swansea Bay

Cefn Cribwr ●

36

● Pencoed

A4229

37

● Bridgend

35

M4

34

Porthcawl ●

● **Cowbridge**

A4265

Llanmihangel ●

Llantwit Major ●

St Athan ●

Cardiff International Airp

Bristol Channel

N

Scale
Kilometres
0 2 4 6 8 10
0 1 2 3 4 5 6
Miles

Key

National Park

Wales border

Hereford

A465

A479

Llanthony

A466

40

A40

Llanfihangel Crucorney

A465

Skirrid Fawr

A465

Lantilio Crossenny

Brynmawr

Abergavenny

B4233

Monmouth

edegar

Ebbw Vale

Blaenavon

hymney

Llanover

A40

Raglan

Trellech

Goytre Wharf

Goetre

Abertillery

B4246

Usk

Wye Valley

9

New Tredegar

A4042

Bargoed

Pontypool

elson

A449

Tintern

Ystrad Mynach

A4051

Cwmbran

A466

Chepstow

Llantarnam

A48

22

Caerleon

Caerwent

Caerphilly

A467

26

25

24

M4

23

M48

27

ffs Well

ngwynlais

M4

28

Newport

Second Severn Crossing

30

29

2

A470

A48

Mouth of the Severn

M5

St Fagan's

Cardiff

Penarth

B4267

arry

South Wales Valleys

These cauldrons of industry and culture give us
Blaenavon World Heritage Site, Rhondda Heritage
Park, Caerphilly Castle, Llancaiach Fawr Manor,
the Monmouthshire and Brecon Canal, Llantarnam
Abbey, Blaenavon Book Town, the Cordell Museum,
the Parc and Dare Miners' Institute and
Cyfarthfa Castle.

Aberdare

Coliseum Theatre. Built in 1937, this striking building nestles in the residential Mount Pleasant Street in Aberdare. The auditorium is distinctive, with its acoustic nodules and intriguing wall friezes. The programme includes music and drama of all kinds, including productions by local community groups and schools.
• Aberdare is on the A4059, which extends north-westward from the A470 north of Pontypridd.
Phone: 01685 881188

Cynon Valley Museum. On the outskirts of Aberdare, you will find this museum of local social history, which also has a contemporary arts and crafts gallery with a changing exhibition programme. There is a café and a shop specialising in design-led jewellery, ceramics and glass.
• On the outskirts of the town, ten minutes' walk from the train and bus stations.
Phone: 01685 886729
www.cynonvalley.co.uk/cv_museum

Above: **Rhondda Valley.**
The village of Cwmparc nestles in the hills surrounding the Rhondda Valley. This landscape, and the coal that came from under it, shaped and developed many of the villages and towns in the South Wales Valleys, including Cwmparc.

Abertillery

St Illtyd's Church, Abertillery.
This restored medieval church is
a reminder that the history of this
part of Wales is not exclusively to
do with coal mining; there were
people here long before that
particular industry boomed.
The simple exterior and
enchanting interior of the
church reflect the spiritual
intentions of its builders, the
white-robed Cistercian monks
of nearby Llantarnam Abbey.
• From J28 on the M4, head
northward on the A467, or drive
southward on the same road
from the A465 at Brynmawr.
Phone: 01495 355537
www.illtyd.abelalways.co.uk

Blaenavon

**Blaenavon UNESCO World
Heritage Site.** Built in the 1780s,
the Blaenavon ironworks was at
the cutting edge of the new
technology that made the
Industrial Revolution possible.
A row of five blast furnaces,
powered by steam, was served
by an ingenious water-balanced
system for transporting iron ore,
coal and limestone into their
open tops. Molten iron ran down
to be cast into rows of 'pigs' in
the yard below. Next to this place
of hot and strenuous labour are
the cottages of **Stack Square**,
where workers lived in the
shadow of the tall chimney.
• Go northward from Newport

on the A4042, then take the A4043 from Pontypool, or head over the Blorenge mountain on the B4246 from Abergavenny.
Phone: 01495 792615
www.world-heritage-blaenavon.org.uk

Big Pit: National Coal Museum.
Situated within the **Blaenavon World Heritage Site**, Big Pit is a deep coalmine where you may descend three hundred feet underground in the cage that once took the miners to work. A former collier will explain to you, from first-hand experience, what life was like for the thousands of men who once toiled at the coal face. Big Pit won the Gulbenkian Prize for Museum of the Year in 2005.
• The industrial heritage sites

of Blaenavon are a substantial distance apart and it is best to drive between them or join a tour.
Phone: 01495 790311
www.museumwales.ac.uk

Above left: **Big Pit: National Coal Museum.** The pithead winding gear, once a common sight throughout the mining valleys, continues to operate at this exciting museum.
Above right: **Cynon Valley Museum.** Learn about the social history of this highly populated and industrious region, including the tough working conditions and legendary camaraderie of the coal-mining communities.

Blaenavon Community Heritage and Cordell Museum. The **World Heritage Site of Blaenavon** is home to this substantial museum, where the displays will guide you through the history of the town from the Industrial Revolution to the modern day. The novelist Alexander Cordell wrote evocatively of life in this corner of Wales, and his desk, personal effects and typewriter may be seen here. Following the inspiration of Hay-on-Wye, Blaenavon's new role as a book town means that you will find a treasure trove of books old and new in its specialist shops.
• The museum is located in the town centre and within reach of the bookshops.
Phone: 01495 790991
www.world-heritage-blaenavon.org.uk

Brynmawr

Brinore Tramroad. This is the eight-mile tram route, near Brynmawr, built in 1815 to link the enormous limestone quarry at Trefil to the **Monmouthshire and Brecon Canal** at Talybont.
• Take a minor road northward from the A465, three miles west of Brynmawr.
www.brinore-tramroad.powys.org.uk

Caerphilly

Caerphilly Castle. This is the largest medieval castle in Wales and, after Windsor and Dover, the third largest in Britain. It was built in the late-13th century by the Anglo-Norman lord of Glamorgan, Gilbert de Clare, to resist attack by supporters of the Welsh Prince Llywelyn. It is a supreme example of 'walls-within-walls' construction. Its water defences are remarkable: the moat widens into lakes that contain three artificial islands, and made the castle virtually impregnable. The famous leaning tower leans at a greater angle than that of Pisa. Look out for days when battle re-enactment societies bring history to life with glinting armour, clashing swords and replicas of ancient siege engines that hurl massive rocks long distances into the moat.
• Caerphilly is just north of Cardiff via the A469 or A470, then A468 from Nantgarw.
www.cadw.wales.gov.uk

Llantarnam

Llantarnam Abbey. Located near Cwmbran, Llantarnam is a working abbey, home to the Sisters of St Joseph of Annecy who welcome visitors by prior arrangement. It was originally built for a Cistercian community of monks in 1179, as a daughter house of Strata Florida.

Left: **Caerphilly Castle.**
The intimidating defences, including the wide moat, would make any but the most determined of attackers think twice. The leaning tower seems to defy gravity.

The remains of the original abbey are built into the present buildings; the large barn is especially impressive.
• From the M4 at J25a or J26, follow signs for Cwmbran to the roundabout on the A4051, then take a minor road signposted to Llantarnam.
Phone: 01633 483232

Merthyr Tydfil

Cyfarthfa Castle. This grand castellated mansion was commissioned by ironmaster William Crawshay in 1824. The area around Merthyr Tydfil and Dowlais was the largest iron-producing centre in the world. Crawshay's Cyfarthfa Ironworks produced cannon and cannon balls for the Royal Navy, including many used by Nelson's ships at Trafalgar in 1805. Large quantities of iron flowed from the furnaces to support the accelerating industrialisation of Britain and to make possible the spread of the emerging railway network. The **Cyfarthfa Castle Museum and Art Gallery** has a fine collection of paintings, decorative items and musical instruments.
• Cyfarthfa Castle is visible in all its grandeur from the A470 south of the junction with the A465 heads-of-the-valleys road, from which it may be reached.
Phone: 01685 723112
www.merthyr.gov.uk

Monmouthshire and Brecon Canal

This scenic canal runs for thirty-two miles (51km) from the **Brecon Beacons** towards **Pontypool** along the **Usk Valley**, and then continues through a mixed rural and industrial landscape to **Newport**. It was built between 1797 and 1812, in an age when roads were notoriously bad, to carry limestone and processed lime from quarries at Trefil and Llangattock, which were linked to it by tramways.
www.waterscape.com

Nelson

Llancaiach Fawr Manor.
Step back in time to 1645 and meet the servants of Colonel Pritchard, owner of this attractive house, as they recount tales about their lives. Listen to their gossip and hear about the customs of over three hundred and fifty years ago. A major topic will be the turmoil of the Civil War raging between King and Parliament. During the early part of the year there was staunch support for the Royalist cause but, following a visit by King Charles in August, the master and his household changed their allegiance in favour of the Parliamentarians.
• Follow signposted minor roads for Nelson and Llancaiach Fawr from the A470 north of

Pontypridd and the A469 north of Caerphilly. Phone: 01443 412248 www.caerphilly.gov.uk

New Tredegar

Elliot Colliery Winding House.
The sight of the massive steam winding engine in action will bring home the scale of the activity and the danger of going underground. At its peak, Elliot Colliery, owned by the Powell Duffryn Steam Coal Company, employed around 2,800 people and produced over a million tons of high-quality steam coal each year.
• Some ten miles north of Caerphilly, off the A469. Phone: 01443 822666 www.caerphilly.gov.uk

Pontypridd

Rhondda Heritage Park.
The former Lewis Merthyr Colliery at Trehafod, at the gateway to the Rhondda valley, is now an entertaining and educational museum of coal mining. The looming presence of the pithead winding gear, surrounded by terraces of colliers' houses spreading up the hillsides, was once the

---

Above: **Llancaiach Fawr.**
Re-enactments of daily life are a popular attraction at this historic house. You can rely on the servants to spill the latest gossip about the master and his family!

defining feature of the densely populated mining towns that grew along the valleys from the mid-19th century onwards.
• Just west of Pontypridd on the A4058.
Phone: 01443 682036
www.rhonddaheritagepark.com

The Muni Arts Centre. In this beautiful converted church in the centre of Pontypridd, you can enjoy a programme of all kinds of music, exhibitions, dance, comedy, puppetry, productions by community groups, and events for children and young people. The venue also includes the Footlights Cafe Bar and the Gallery Shop.

• Programmes are available from the centre, local shops and library or via the Arts Council of Wales website.
Phone: 01443 485934
www.muniartscentre.co.uk

Tredegar

Sirhowy Ironworks. This site at Tredegar is a rare survivor of the early iron industry: the carefully conserved buildings date back to 1778. In 1818, the works were acquired by one James Harford of Ebbw Vale and began operating as a supplier to the Ebbw Vale Ironworks in the next valley to the east. Sirhowy provided pig iron that was worked into wrought iron and later, from the end of the

19th century, into steel.

• Five miles north-east of Merthyr Tydfil, take the Dukestown exit from the A4048 Tredegar bypass – past a petrol station and through a gap in the terrace of houses.

Phone: 01495 355537
www.blaenau-gwent.gov.uk

....

Treorchy

The Parc and Dare Theatre.
This magnificent building, towering above the terraces of Treorchy, was built in 1913. It was funded by the workers of the Park and Dare collieries, who donated a penny for each pound of their wages so that they and their families could benefit from the cultural and educational opportunities provided by a miners' institute. It is home to the famous Treorchy male-voice choir, the multiple-prizewinning Parc and Dare Band and Rhondda Cynon Taff Community Arts. Top international musicians also grace the vigorous programme.

• This fine building towers over the terraces of Treorchy, in the Rhondda valley north-west of

---

Above: **Rhondda Heritage Park.**
One of the top heritage attractions in the Valleys, the Rhondda Heritage Park includes a multi-media exhibition, museum, art gallery and shop – as well as a tour to experience the working conditions in the Lewis Merthyr Colliery during the 1950s.

Pontypridd, and is visible for miles around.
Phone: 01443 773112
www.rhondda-cynon-taff.gov.uk

Mining Valleys. The names of the mining towns – Porth, Tonypandy, Treorchy, Treherbert, Blaenrhondda, Maerdy, Ferndale, Llwynypia – resonate with the memory of the hard times endured by these close-knit communities. The memorial at Llwynypia, depicting a miner and his family, is especially moving.
www.rhondda-cynon-taff.gov.uk

Festivals and events

The Big Cheese. Set in the shadows of one of Europe's largest castles, Caerphilly Castle, The Big Cheese held in **July** is an extravaganza of street entertainers, living history encampments, music, dance and traditional funfair, portraying the history, heritage and culture of Caerphilly.
• www.caerphilly.gov.uk/visiting

The Big Balloon. Balloons of all shapes, sizes and colours gather at the Blackwood Showfields over the **August** Bank Holiday weekend for the Big Balloon Festival. The highlight of the weekend is the nightglow and

fireworks display which takes place on the Sunday evening.
• www.caerphilly.gov.uk/visiting

demonstrations, animal displays and food and craft stalls.
• www.rhondda-cynon-taff.gov.uk

Jazz in the Park. Jazz in the Park is held annually in **September** in the beautiful surroundings of Pontypool Park. The event includes international stars as well as local bands and attracts thousands of Jazz lovers.
• www.torfaenjazz.org

The Big Welsh Bite. Held in **August** at Pontypridd's Ynysangharad Memorial Park, The Big Welsh Bite is a food and agricultural event which takes as its theme 'Food and Agriculture through the Ages.' The weekend event has celebrity chef cooking

Above left: **The Big Balloon.** Spectacular mass balloon launches, live music, displays, stalls and white knuckle rides all make for a fantastic weekend.
Above right: **The Big Cheese.** Enjoy folk dancing, falconry, fire eating and minstrels at Caerphilly's big three-day festival each July.

Cardiff and Vale of Glamorgan

Experience capital and countryside in harmony as you savour multicultural Cardiff, the Millennium Stadium, Castell Coch, Llandaff Cathedral, the Wales Millennium Centre, St Fagans National History Museum, St David's Hall, the Norwegian Church Cultural Centre and Cowbridge.

Barry

Cold Knap. This site dates from the latter days of the Roman presence in Wales during the 3rd and 4th centuries, and is believed to have been a small naval depot and coastal settlement served by a ferry. Nearby **Cold Knap Farm**, built in the 16th century, is the oldest house in Barry.
• From Barry's redeveloped waterfront, follow signs to Barry Island and Cold Knap.
www.barrywales.co.uk

Barry. The town of Barry grew to prominence around the docks that David Davies of Llandinam built to serve his coal mines, in competition with the docks of Cardiff. Down at the redeveloped waterfront there is a fine statue of him studying the plans for his docks; an identical statue, far away from the sea, is sited in his home village.
www.barrywales.co.uk

Bridgend

Newcastle Hill. Now a conservation area, this oldest part of Bridgend is centred on the remains of the castle and the character-filled streets of cottages surrounding it. Amongst

Above: **Cardiff.** Few cities have so much green space, and such attractive civic buildings, as Cardiff – the Civic Centre is on the left and the castle is at lower right.

the older buildings is **St John's Hospice**, where weary pilgrims would rest on their way to **St David's** in Pembrokeshire. Leaflets are available for self-guided walks.

• Bridgend is accessible by J35/J36 of the M4.

Brynmenyn

Bryngarw House. A couple of miles north of Bridgend, you will find this fine country house with its smartly furnished rooms, standing in 113 acres of parkland. There is a visitor centre and exhibition, along with a children's play area and the Harlequin restaurant.

• North of Bridgend, a couple of miles from J36 of the M4

motorway. Phone: 01656 729009
www.bridgend.gov.uk

Cardiff

Cardiff Civic Centre. The majestic Portland stone buildings of the Civic Centre were designed as statements of civic pride by the Edwardian city fathers who steered Cardiff's development into the world's busiest coal port. **City Hall** – with its tall clock tower, graceful Renaissance embellishments and a dome topped by a fierce looking coiled dragon – was under construction when Cardiff gained city status in 1905. Upstairs, there are fine statues of famous figures from Welsh history. Other buildings in the group include the **Crown**

Courts, the **National Museum Cardiff**, executive offices of the **National Assembly for Wales**, the **Temple of Peace** (home to the **Welsh Centre for International Affairs**) and several departments of **Cardiff University**.
• Cardiff's Civic Centre is prominent as you approach the city centre by road from the north. www.cardiff.gov.uk

Multicultural Cardiff.
The proportion of people whose families originated from elsewhere in the world is, as one would expect, greater in the seaport city of Cardiff than in other parts of Wales.
The **Butetown History and Arts Centre** tells the story of how the docklands of Tiger Bay became one of Britain's most cosmopolitan communities.
The **MAS Carnival** brings the exuberance of the Caribbean and Rio de Janeiro to Cardiff Bay each summer. The world's major religions enjoy an atmosphere of mutual respect in the city. Cardiff's twelve mosques serve the large Muslim community, and Jewish, Afro-Caribbean, Chinese,

Above left: **Civic Centre.** The fine Portland stone buildings of Cardiff's Civic Centre have been compared to the similarly emphatic architectural expressions of civic pride to be found in Washington DC and New Delhi.
Above right: **MAS Carnival.**
Hundreds of people in flamboyant costumes, masks and head pieces dance Mardi Gras style through the streets of Cardiff Bay.

Hindu, Sikh and Buddhist communities meet at their respective centres, invigorated by Cardiff's popularity with students from all parts of the globe.

• Butetown History and Arts Centre is in Bute Street, close to Cardiff Bay rail station.
Phone: 029 2025 6757
www.bhac.org

Cardiff Castle. Each phase of this marvellous site's evolution over the past two thousand years is accessible. The Romans established a fort here, the foundations of which have been incorporated into the castle's outer walls. The Normans showed who was boss by building the intimidating keep. In Tudor times, the Herbert family lived in style in their mansion. During the 1860s, the eccentric Victorian architect William Burges transformed the Third Marquess of Bute's home into one of the most extravagant examples of Gothic Revival fantasy to be found anywhere.

• Follow signs from the M4 to the city centre and convenient pay-and-display car parks.
Phone: 029 2087 8100
www.cardiffcastle.com

Left and above: **Cardiff Castle.** At Cardiff Castle, visit the Norman Keep and the amazingly ornate home of the Bute family.

Welch Regiment Museum at Cardiff Castle. Displays of uniforms, weapons, medals and memorabilia commemorate the services of the Welch Regiment, which was founded in 1719 and absorbed into the Royal Regiment of Wales in 1969. The support given to the regular battalions by the Glamorgan militia and auxiliary land forces – including the Infantry, the Rifle Volunteers and the Yeomanry Cavalry – is recorded. The museum shop has a good range of books and regimental souvenirs.
• You may visit the museum, the main castle buildings and the grounds separately.
Phone: 029 2022 9367
www.rrw.org.uk

Llandaff Cathedral. Occupying a site that has been sacred since the 6th century, Llandaff Cathedral blends a Victorian structure with modern additions, including the sublime sculpture Christ in Majesty by Sir Jacob Epstein, and the Welch Regiment Memorial Chapel, dedicated to St David. In addition to being a place of worship, the cathedral also hosts concerts and exhibitions.
• Cardiff's Cathedral Road, across the River Taff from the castle, leads to Llandaff village.
Phone: 029 2056 4554
www.llandaffcathedral.org.uk

Millennium Stadium. Located in the centre of Cardiff, this is the shrine of the national game,

rugby. Emotions run high when the team sprints out from the tunnel, to thunderous applause and cheering, to join in the national anthem and to be inspired to great feats of skill and bravery by the sound of tens of thousands of supporters singing the favourite hymns of their homeland. For many people, the cultural identity of Wales is inseparable from the game of rugby. For them, it is part of the heart and soul of the nation and – at least when the team is doing well – a source of national pride on a world stage.

• The Millennium Stadium and Cardiff Rugby Club are next door to each other, between the river and the city centre.
Phone: 029 2082 2228

(stadium tours)
www.millenniumstadium.com

City venues. As befits a capital city, Cardiff has a wealth of cultural venues to suit all tastes. The **Cardiff International Arena** (Phone: 029 2022 4488) can seat up to five thousand people and is the main venue for rock and pop music, and for the really big international stars. Cardiff-born Shirley Bassey has raised the roof there on numerous occasions.

Above left: **Llandaff Cathedral.** The striking interior of Llandaff Cathedral is an inspiring combination of restored Victorian Gothic and 20th-century styles. Above right: **St David's Hall.** Classical concerts are among the many events held here.

The **New Theatre** (Phone: 029 2087 8889), a traditional Edwardian playhouse dating from 1906, puts on high-calibre drama, dance, musicals and pantomime. The **Sherman Theatre** (Phone: 029 2064 6900) nurtures tomorrow's talent by staging new plays and promoting youth projects. **Cardiff University's School of Music**, and the **Royal Welsh College of Music and Drama** present frequent public performances. **The Gate** (Phone: 029 2048 3344) and **Llanover Hall** (Phone: 029 2063 1144) are community arts centres especially popular for their classes and workshops.
• Llanover Hall is in Canton, across the river from the city centre. The Gate is in Roath. All other venues are in the city centre.

St David's Hall. Conveniently situated at the heart of Cardiff's city centre, St David's Hall is the National Concert Hall of Wales. Its pleasant auditorium accommodates a wide range of entertainment, including classical music, pop, rock, folk, jazz, world music, comedy, film and dance, along with exhibitions and conferences. World-class concerts feature the **BBC National Orchestra of Wales** as well as many famous visiting orchestras, chamber ensembles, soloists and conductors.
The **Welsh Proms** concerts provide an uplifting celebration of classical music each summer.
The biennial **BBC Cardiff Singer of the World** competition is a respected launch pad for future international stars of opera house and recital stage.
• Overlooking The Hayes, at the heart of Cardiff's shopping centre. Phone: 029 2087 8444 www.stdavidshallcardiff.co.uk

Chapter Arts. Chapter has an international reputation for excellence, innovation and collaboration and much of the social and creative life in Cardiff revolves around this arts centre. Chapter Arts is the flagship for contemporary arts in Wales. Its ever-changing programme of the best performances, films and exhibitions from Wales and around the world makes it one of the largest arts complexes of its kind in Europe.
• As well as a theatre, two cinema screens and exhibition rooms, Chapter Arts has a gift shop and excellent café and bar. Chapter Arts is situated in Canton. Phone: 029 2030 4400 www.chapter.org

City centre galleries. The artistic scene in Cardiff is thriving. As well the world renowned galleries of the **National Museum Cardiff**, the city centre boasts a number

Left: **Millennium Stadium.** Since opening in June 1999, this world-class venue has welcomed over 1.3 million visitors each year. It has the first retractable roof in the UK and is used for major sporting events and concerts.

of Wales's best contemporary art galleries. The **Albany Gallery** is long-established and recognised as one of Wales's most successful privately-owned commercial galleries. Its monthly exhibition programme includes leading Welsh and British artists. The **Martin Tinney Gallery** specialises in Welsh and Wales-based artists of the highest quality and the **Kooywood Gallery**, established in 2004, is a forum for established and new artists to display and sell their art and covers a wide range of visual arts including paintings, sculptures, ceramics, glass and photography.

• **Albany Gallery**, Albany Road. Phone: 029 2048 7158
www.albanygallery.com
Martin Tinney Gallery, St Andrews Crescent.
Phone: 029 2064 1411
www.artwales.com
Kooywood Gallery, Museum Place. Phone: 029 2023 5093
www.kooywoodgallery.com

National Museum Cardiff. In fascinating displays about history, science and art, this fine building houses vast collections of material including rocks, minerals and fossils; prehistoric and Celtic artefacts; five centuries' worth of paintings, sculpture and decorative art; and natural history specimens ranging from Snowdonia's delicate arctic-alpine plants to the skeleton of a whale. Highlights include superb Impressionist and Post-

Impressionist paintings by Monet, Renoir, Cézanne, Van Gogh and others. These were given to the museum by the sisters Gwendoline and Margaret Davies, beneficiaries of the fortune derived from coal mines, railways and Barry Docks by their grandfather, David Davies of Llandinam. The international Artes Mundi visual-art competition is held at the museum in even-numbered years, when conceptual works of outstanding imagination are displayed. As with all National Museum Wales locations, admission is free.

• As you face the impressive Civic Centre, the National Museum Cardiff is the building to the right – **City Hall**, in the middle, is also worth a look, for its fine paintings and statues of historical figures. Phone: 029 2039 7951 www.museumwales.ac.uk

Cardiff Bay

Impressive listed buildings and preserved dockland fixtures lend historical integrity to the redeveloped waterfront of Cardiff Bay. During the second half of the 19th century, as a consequence of the coal-mining boom in the

Left and above: **National Museum Cardiff.** There is a year-round programme of talks, workshops and activities for all ages at the museum, including opportunities to learn about the superb collection of French Impressionist paintings.

valleys to the north, Cardiff grew rapidly as a seaport and centre of commerce, and was granted city status in 1905. By 1913, this was the world's largest coal-exporting port, drawing in a cosmopolitan population that formed the foundation of today's vibrantly multicultural city.
• Prominently signed from J33 on the M4, and from the city centre.
www.cardiffbay.co.uk

Bay Art. In this modern gallery near the Wales Millennium Centre, you will find for sale a tremendous selection of high-quality contemporary art in many media. Regular exhibitions feature the best amongst established and emerging painters, sculptors, printers, ceramicists, jewellers and others. See programme for workshops, seminars and artist interviews.
• 54B/C Bute Street
Phone: 029 2065 0016
www.bayart.org.uk

Norwegian Church Cultural Centre. This picturesque former church was built to serve the spiritual needs of Norwegian seafarers whose ships brought in timber to make pit props for the

---

Above: **Cardiff Bay.** Historic docklands have been transformed into a high-quality leisure, business and cultural environment.
Right: **Norwegian Church.** A dramatic statue of Captain Scott stands near this attractive cultural venue.

coal mines inland. It is now a popular venue for music, literary events and exhibitions of painting and photography. Some of its events have Scandinavian themes and are organised in partnership with Cardiff's twin region of Hordaland in Norway. The author Roald Dahl was born in Cardiff in 1916 to Norwegian parents (his father was a shipbroker) and was baptised in this church.

• At Cardiff Bay's Inner Harbour, near the Wales Millennium Centre. Phone: 029 2045 4899

National Assembly for Wales Building. The sixty members of the National Assembly for Wales meet to discuss and vote upon policy in this striking building overlooking Cardiff Bay. In a gesture of faith that the National Assembly's powers might evolve further, the new building has been named the Senedd, the Welsh word for a senate or parliament. The circular Debating Chamber is intended to encourage the politicians to work in a constructive spirit of co-operation; their deliberations may be viewed from the public gallery above. Illuminated by daylight, the building is a showpiece of high-quality Welsh building materials including

Left and above: **National Assembly for Wales.** There is public access to much of the interior of the building – the transparency of the structure is intentionally symbolic of the openness of the work that goes on there.

Photograph Bill Cooper

wood, steel and slate.

The welcoming staff will quickly help you through the airport-style security system at the entrance and you are then free to explore the public areas, which include a café. The adjacent **Pierhead Building** houses the **National Assembly for Wales Visitor and Education Centre**, where you may learn how in many areas of life Wales is governed regionally, with decision-making devolved from Parliament in London.

• Near the **Wales Millennium Centre**, and close to train and bus services (for Cardiff Bay), a short walk from car parks at **Mermaid Quay** and the **Norwegian Church Cultural Centre**.

Phone: 029 2089 8477

www.wales.gov.uk/assemblybuilding

Wales Millennium Centre.

This landmark building at Cardiff Bay is one of the world's most innovative and dynamic performing arts venues, presenting a programme of entertainment that is second to none. The main Donald Gordon Theatre is a spectacular auditorium with acoustics and

---

Left: **Wales Millennium Centre.** Composed by poet Gwyneth Lewis, the words above the entrance read: "Creu Gwir fel Gwydr o Ffwrnais Awen" – which means "Creating Truth like Glass from Inspiration's Furnace" – and "In these Stones Horizons Sing".

Above: **Magic Flute.** This colourful production is one of many performances from the multi-award winning Welsh National Opera.

capabilities designed to delight performers and audiences alike. Innovative productions in the smaller studio theatre, daily events in the foyer and a selection of bars and restaurants make this a versatile must-see cultural destination. Seven organisations enjoy a synergetic neighbourliness at their bases here: **Welsh National Opera**, **Diversions Dance Company**, **Hijinx Theatre**, **Academi** (the literature promotion agency for Wales), **Touch Trust** (creative therapists), the **Tŷ Cerdd** music information centre and **Urdd Gobaith Cymru**, Wales's leading youth organisation.
• Signed from the city centre and accessible by train, taxi, public bus or Cardiff Tour bus.
Phone: 08700 402000
www.wmc.org.uk

Welsh National Opera. Wales is very fortunate to have its own world-class opera company – Welsh National Opera – which began as an amateur society some sixty years ago and now operates at the highest professional level from its state-of-the-art production base at the **Wales Millennium Centre.** Top international soloists and directors, a highly regarded orchestra and chorus, and skilled technical staff achieve exemplary standards. In addition to presenting a full programme of opera in Cardiff, from classical works to innovative modern productions, the company also goes on tour in the UK.
A programme of community concerts, workshops and

educational activities takes opera to local centres all over Wales.
Phone: 029 2063 5000
www.wno.org.uk

Cowbridge

There was a small town here in Roman times and today's High Street follows the Roman road Via Julia. The town walls and church were built in the 13th century, after which Cowbridge grew into its continuing role as a busy market town. The Grammar School was founded in 1608 and was owned between 1685 and 1918 by Jesus College, Oxford, which many of its pupils attended. Cowbridge is a prosperous, bustling place, famed for having the most upmarket high street of any town in Wales. Its restaurants, wine bars, antique shops and fashion boutiques occupy handsome 18th and 19th century houses and premises built for the merchants of this most attractive of towns.
www.cowbridge.co.uk

Plas Llanmihangel.
This Elizabethan manor house has elements that date back to the 12th century. It is now operated as a guest house but

Above: Cowbridge. The agreeable town of Cowbridge is a thoroughly pleasant place to explore – with its high-quality shops, attractive pubs and restaurants, and numerous historical sites.

there are guided tours for groups by arrangement, complemented by cream teas in the beautiful surroundings.
• A couple of miles south of Cowbridge along narrow country lanes.
Phone: 01446 774610

Llantwit Major

Llanilltyd Fawr. St Illtud founded a church, monastery and missionary centre here towards the end of the 5th century. This was one of the most important sites of the early Celtic church – a place of learning where both St David and St Patrick are believed to have been educated. Ancient Celtic crosses are to be seen in the church and around the churchyard.
• On the Glamorgan Heritage Coast, some five miles south of Cowbridge via the B4270.
www.llantwit-major.net

St Donat's. The medieval St Donat's Castle houses Atlantic College, the world's first international sixth-form college, where you may join guided tours during the holidays each August. The **St Donat's Arts Centre** is the Vale of Glamorgan's largest arts venue and offers a comprehensive programme in all genres.
• St Donat's is west of Llantwit Major: follow the B4270 from Cowbridge.
Phone: 01446 799000
www.atlanticcollege.org

Penarth

On the outskirts of Penarth, you will find the **Cosmeston Medieval Village** – a re-creation of a 14th century settlement where costumed guides will lead you into the past. Art lovers will find much of interest in the town. The **Turner House Art Gallery** displays fine paintings and The **Oriel Washington Gallery** is housed in a striking Art Deco former cinema displaying an exciting selection of work for sale by contemporary artists.
• Turner House Gallery Phone: 029 2070 8870.
Oriel Washington Gallery Phone: 029 2071 2100
www.washingtongallery.co.uk.
Cosmeston is south of Penarth, on the B4267.
www.valeofglamorgan.gov.uk

Penarth promenade and pier.
The elegant Victorian town of Penarth has retained the appeal of its tranquil parks and gardens, its popular promenade and its ornate pier. Restaurants, ice cream parlours, gift shops and galleries pull in the crowds at weekends and holidays. The last seagoing paddle steamer, the Waverley, and the motor vessel Balmoral make numerous calls at the pier during the summer. In the tradition of the old Campbell's White Funnel

Right: National History Museum.
The gardens of St Fagans Castle.

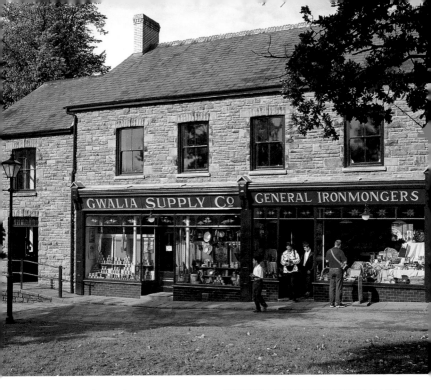

steamers, they take passengers on cruises along the Welsh coast, around the islands of **Steep Holm** and **Flat Holm**, and across to Bristol, Somerset and Devon.
• Follow signs for Cardiff Bay and Penarth from J33 on the M4. www.valeofglamorgan.gov.uk

Porthcawl

Porthcawl Grand Pavilion. This famous venue situated on the promenade is a seafront theatre offering a great programme of shows and concerts.
• South from J37 on the M4, via the A4229. Phone: 01656 786996 www.bridgend.gov.uk

St Fagans

St Fagans National History Museum. Here at one of the world's most impressive open-air museums, you will find more than forty buildings, ranging from a re-created **Celtic village** of two thousand years ago to the eco-friendly **House for the Future.** In beautiful parkland surrounding **St Fagans Castle**, authentic buildings – including farmhouses, barns, workers' cottages, village shops, a miners' institute, a woollen mill, a chapel and a church – have been transported stone by stone from all over Wales and meticulously rebuilt. The indoor galleries illuminate the social and cultural life of

Wales through artefacts and costumes. Craft demonstrators around the site explain their skills as you watch. Events include celebrations at May Day and Christmas.
• Just south of J33 on the M4, regular bus services to St Fagans village. Phone: 029 2057 3500
www.museumwales.ac.uk

St Nicholas

Dyffryn Gardens. These Grade I listed Edwardian landscaped gardens are among the largest and finest in Wales. Located between Cowbridge and Cardiff, they are a popular location for open-air concerts and theatre productions.

• Just south of St Nicholas, on the A48 west of Cardiff.
Phone: 029 2059 3328
www.dyffryngardens.org.uk

Taff's Well

Just north of Cardiff, the hot spring that gave its name to the village that grew around it has been known for its healing properties since Roman times.

Above: **National History Museum.** The many attractions of this special place include traditional dancing on May Day, restored houses from all over Wales, the gardens and interiors of St Fagans Castle, educational activities for adults and children, and the atmospheric Gwalia Supply Company store.

It has been neglected for many years but there are plans to restore it to use. Analysis of the water has shown it to have a similar mineral content to the springs at Bath.

• From J32 on the M4, the A470's busy junctions and sliproads lead to Taff's Well.
www.rhondda-cynon-taff.gov.uk

Tongwynlais

The eccentric Victorian architect William Burges designed **Castell Coch** as a retreat for the Third Marquess of Bute and his family, though they spent little time here. Burges was inspired by chateaux in Switzerland and France to build an idealised reconstruction of the medieval castle of Gilbert the Red, Earl of Gloucester, which originally stood on this elevated site overlooking the Taff gorge at Tongwynlais. The exuberant interior is decorated with a riot of symbolic imagery derived from Classical mythology, Aesop's fables and medieval manuscripts, along with an eclectic assemblage of French, Gothic and Moorish influences.

• At Tongwynlais, within sight of J32 of the M4.
Phone: 029 2081 0101
www.cadw.wales.gov.uk

Vale of Glamorgan

The north-western part of the Vale of Glamorgan region extends towards the Valleys and includes the town of Maesteg and the

upper part of the Ogmore valley. **Maesteg Town Hall** is a splendidly old-fashioned and homely building where you can enjoy concerts, drama and exhibitions. The **Blaengarw Workmen's Hall**, at the top of the Garw valley, is a cinema, theatre and dance venue. The **Berwyn Centre** at Nant y Moel is a theatre and exhibition centre.

• Head northward from J36 on the M4 to this region of industry and vigorous culture.

Festivals and events

Festivals. The **Cardiff Festival** is said to be Europe's biggest free festival, attracting upwards of five hundred thousand people to arts, music, theatre and comedy events at venues throughout the city, including its parks and streets. The **International Festival of Musical Theatre** is held every two years, alternating with **Cardiff Singer of the World**,

Above left: **Dyffryn Gardens.** The Vale of Glamorgan is a haven of rural peace and Dyffryn Gardens is a special oasis of tranquillity where you will find formal gardens and open parkland that will revive the spirits in any season.

Above right: **Castell Coch.** A magical sight from the M4 just north of Cardiff, Castell Coch gives a convincing impression of a medieval fantasy castle. William Burges was able to let his imagination run riot, with no concern about cost, when he designed the astonishing rooms at Castell Coch.

and brings the best of musical theatre to the **Wales Millennium Centre**, the **New Theatre** and other venues. Down around the waterfront, the **Worldport Festival** celebrates Cardiff's role as a seaport by inviting world music performers to historic venues including **The Coal Exchange** – where many deals were agreed during the coal port's heyday – and **The Point**, a former church. **Gŵyl Ifan**, the UK's biggest folk-dancing festival, brings dance groups from the Celtic nations to Cardiff's city centre each June.
www.cardiff-festival.com

The **St Donat's Music Festival**, early each **September**, is a celebration of music by living composers.
• St Donat's is west of Llantwit Major: follow the B4270 from Cowbridge.
Phone: 01446 799000
www.atlanticcollege.org

Cardiff International Food & Drink Festival.
A key ingredient of the Cardiff Festival, the Cardiff International Food & Drink Festival, held in **July**, is a free food-lovers' paradise promoting the very finest in food, drink and entertainment from Wales and elsewhere, held at Roald Dahl's Plass, just in front of the Wales Millennium Centre.
• Phone: 029 2087 2087
www.cardiff-festival.com

Heritage Weekend. The Heritage Weekend is held every **September** at Cosmeston Medieval Village, near Penarth. The buildings and costumed demonstrators recreate the year 1350, a troubled time in relations between Wales and England. Events include re-enactments, storytelling and archery.

• Cosmeston Medieval Village also organise events throughout the year – check with the local Tourist Information Centre for events and dates.
Phone: 029 2070 1678

Barry Waterfront Tall Ships Festival. Barry's newly developed waterfront is home to the annual Tall Ships Festival held in early September. As well as a number of impressive tall ships there are craft and food stalls, fairground rides, street entertainers, live bands and steam train rides.
• Phone: 01446 747171

Above left: **Cardiff Festival.** At the heart of the Cardiff Festival is the very best of street theatre, live music, youth and children's entertainment, funfairs, food and drama. The Festival finishes with The Big Weekend – a three-day event with live outdoor music and funfair.
Above right: **WNO concert.** Cardiff Bay hosts open-air concerts by big names: this is Welsh National Opera.

Wye Valley and Vale of Usk

Follow Turner and Wordsworth to these vales of heritage and see Tintern Abbey, Offa's Dyke, the Monmouthshire and Brecon Canal, Abergavenny, Monmouth, Tredegar House, the National Roman Legion Museum, Usk Rural Life Museum, Llantilio Crossenny Festival and the Newport Riverfront Theatre.

Abergavenny

With a centre full of character reflecting its origins as a medieval market town, Abergavenny is an attractive place to explore.

The **Abergavenny Museum**, housed in a hunting lodge within the walls of the castle, has reconstructions of a Victorian kitchen, a saddler's workshop and a 1950s grocery store.

• Well connected to the M4 and M50/M5 by the A40 and A449 dual carriageways.
www.abergavenny.co.uk

Caerleon

Known to the Romans as Isca, this is one of the most revealing of their settlements to have been excavated anywhere in Europe. They built a large military base here, with barracks for the 5,500 members of the Second Augustan Legion. The adjacent township had an **amphitheatre** and a bath house – a leisure centre, in effect, with open-air swimming pool, covered exercise hall and a series of hot, warm and cold baths.

The historical significance of Caerleon, one of the three

Above: **Caerleon Roman Amphitheatre.** There are authentic re-enactments here, each summer, of Roman military tactics.

principal military bases of Roman Britannia, is reflected at the **Roman Legionary Museum**. Here you will find a reconstruction of a barrack room and fascinating displays of decorative art, weapons, domestic artefacts and architectural fragments, and even some gemstones lost by customers at the baths.

Also in Caerleon, the sculpture trail is a permanent legacy of the **International Sculpture and Arts Festival**, held each July, and the **Ffwrwm Art and Crafts Centre** is well worth a visit.

• Brown signs on the M4 point to this site of European importance just north of Newport. www.caerleon.net

Caerwent

This was the Roman provincial capital, Venta Silurum, and the first town in Wales. It was founded in 75 AD after the territory of the local Silurian people was brought under control. Its street grid and amenities, including a basilica, forum, bath houses, shops and temples, evolved over the following three hundred years of Roman occupation. The town walls, up to sixteen feet (5m) high, remain impressive. At the height of its prosperity, the population of Venta Silurum, which means Market of the Silures, was probably around 2,500 – far greater than any other

place in Wales would reach for some fifteen hundred years.
• Take the A48 from J24 of the M4, or from J2 on the M48, then left at the approach to Chepstow.

Chepstow

Chepstow Castle. The solid castle and remnants of the town walls underline Chepstow's importance as a strategic frontier settlement.
Chepstow Museum, situated in an elegant 18th century house, covers the town's history as a port and market centre. There are displays on the wine trade, boatbuilding and salmon fishing.
St Mary's Church Walk is a charming old street of quaint architecture and small shops; look out for the Art on the

Railings events each summer.
• Reached via the M48 and the original Severn Bridge, not the M4 – or by the scenic Wye valley from Monmouth.
Phone: 01291 624065
www.cadw.wales.gov.uk

Above left: **Caerleon Roman Amphitheatre**. Excavations at Caerleon's amphitheatre, barracks and baths have revealed valuable insights into the Roman occupation of Britain two millennia ago.
Above right: **Chepstow Castle**. Perched high above the banks of the river Wye, this castle was constructed only a year after the Norman conquest of 1066.

Offa's Dyke. King Offa of Mercia ordered the building of this earthwork not so much as a means of defence but as a line of demarcation between his territory and the vigorously defended kingdoms and princedoms of Wales to the west, which the Saxons never conquered. It has stood since the 8th century, and for much of its 182-mile length continues to be visible close to the border between Wales and England. The **Offa's Dyke Path National Trail** may be followed all the way from the estuary of the River Wye, near Chepstow, to Prestatyn on the north Wales coast.

• Maps and guidebooks are available from the Tourist Information Centre near Chepstow Castle.
www.offasdyke.demon.co.uk

Border castles. William Fitz Osbern, a supporter of William the Conqueror, started work on **Chepstow Castle** soon after 1066 to guard the strategic crossing point over the River Wye. The Normans soon consolidated their occupation of this corner of Wales. The numerous castles of this region, including **Abergavenny, Caldicot, Grosmont, Skenfrith, White Castle, Monmouth, Usk, Penhow and Raglan,** tell a story of increasingly stable and peaceful times as intimidating fortresses were superseded by the precursors of more comfortable country houses.

• Minor roads (B4347, B4233, B4521) north-west of Monmouth lead to Skenfrith, Grosmont and White Castle.
www.cadw.wales.gov.uk

....

Goytre Wharf

Call at this informative visitor centre on the **Monmouthshire and Brecon Canal** to learn how this scenic waterway was built to link Brecon and Newport. Tramways gave access from it to nearby quarries and to the ironworks of Blaenavon. Transportation by canal barge was the most efficient way of taking limestone and processed lime down to the docks at Newport, for export to other parts of Britain or overseas.

• Near Llanover, off the A4042 – there are scenic stretches of canal between here and Abergavenny.
Phone: 01873 881069
www.waterscape.com

Above left: **Offa's Dyke.** This is the linear earthwork that approximately marks the boundary between England and Wales. It consists of a ditch and rampart. As originally constructed, it must have been about 27 metres wide and 8 metres from the ditch bottom to the bank top.
Above right: **Monmouthshire and Brecon Canal.** One of the most beautiful cruising waterways in Britain, completely isolated from the rest of the canal system.

Llanthony

Llanthony Priory. It was here that St David embarked upon his ascetic life as a hermit – drinking only water and eating only the wild leeks that would, as a consequence, become the emblem of Wales. The Priory, founded for Augustinian canons in 1107, is a haven of tranquillity amid wondrous scenery.

The church is aligned with the position on the ridge where the sun rises on St David's day, the 1st of March.

• From the A465, north of Abergavenny, follow narrow roads from Llanfihangel Crucorney.
www.cadw.wales.gov.uk

Skirrid Fawr. This distinctively shaped peak near Abergavenny has been considered a holy mountain for centuries: the Archangel Michael is said to have appeared here and there are remains of a sacred building on the cleft summit. This is where, during the Protestant Reformation, persecuted Catholics would meet in secret to celebrate Mass, at great risk to their lives.

• There are marked footpaths from the A465 and B4521 north of Abergavenny.
www.abergavenny.co.uk

Monmouth

Two fine statues overlook Monmouth's **Agincourt Square.** Henry V secured victory at that crucial battle through the services of archers from this part of the Welsh Borders. Charles Stewart Rolls, descended from a Monmouthshire family, teamed up with Henry Royce to found the famous manufacturers of aircraft engines and cars. Also in Monmouth, the hilltop site of The Kymin encompasses a circular two-storey banqueting house and a small temple dedicated to the glories of the Royal Navy; Nelson visited it in 1802. As is the case in so many historic towns throughout Wales, Monmouth makes the most of its cultural attributes. The **Nelson Museum** has one of the world's best collections of material relating to the legendary Admiral.
The centrally located **Local History Museum, Monmouth Castle**, the **Regimental Museum** and the **Wyastone Leys Concert Hall**, just up the A499 from the town, contribute to the mix.
• www.monmouth.org.uk

Above: **Llanthony Priory.**
Go carefully along the narrow roads that lead to Llanthony Priory, in its serene surroundings.

Newport

The city of Newport stands at the mouth of the Usk, where it grew as a port serving the eastern valleys of the south Wales coalfield. Its **Transporter Bridge**, opened in 1906, is a triumph of engineering. People and cars are carried over in a gondola suspended beneath a structure tall enough for ships to pass beneath. The City of Newport is rich in cultural attractions. The **Riverfront Theatre and Arts Centre**, just along the bank of the Usk from the ruins of the castle, is a superbly equipped modern theatre presenting a wealth of entertainment. The medieval ship uncovered when its foundations were dug, and the bones of an Iron Age man found below the ship, are being conserved for display. **Newport Museum and Art Gallery** exhibits material from Roman Caerwent and chronicles the Chartist Uprising. Just north of Newport, where a flight of locks raises the Monmouthshire and Brecon Canal 168 feet (51m) in half a mile (0.8km), the **Fourteen Locks Canal Centre** illustrates the growth and decline of water transport, and the industries it served since 1796.
• The city of Newport is mid-way between Cardiff and the Second Severn Crossing.
www.newport.gov.uk

St Woolo's Cathedral.
Overlooking Newport from its hilltop site, this is the cathedral of the diocese of Monmouth. Its rather curious name is a corruption of Gwynllyw, the Welsh name of the 5th century saint who first ministered here. The Most Reverend Dr Rowan Williams served here as Bishop of Monmouth and Archbishop of Wales, before becoming Archbishop of Canterbury.
• The cathedral is a short drive or a moderate walk from Newport's city centre.
www.newport.gov.uk

Tredegar House.
Set in ninety acres of gardens and parkland, this outstanding example of Restoration architecture was the ancestral home of the Morgan family for more than five hundred years. Discover what life was like, both above and below stairs, as you tour the magnificent staterooms decorated with ornate carving, gilding and fine

Above left: **Riverfront Theatre and Arts Centre.** When the foundations for this attractive centre were excavated in 2002, the discovery of the remains of a 15th century trading vessel – believed to be from south-western France or northern Iberia – was a wonderful boost to Newport's new status as a city.
Above right: **Transporter Bridge.** Designed by the French engineer Ferdinand Arnodin, Newport's remarkable Transporter Bridge has been carrying vehicles over the river Usk since 1906.

paintings, and the fascinating domestic quarters. The stable blocks house some excellent craft shops.

• Tredegar House is close to J28 on the M4, just west of Newport. Phone: 01633 815880 www.newport.gov.uk

························

Tintern

The ruins of the magnificent Cistercian abbey of Tintern, founded in 1131, stand in a place of sublime beauty where the River Wye cuts through a narrow limestone gorge overlooked by 600-foot cliffs. The roof is gone and the interior is bare, but it is still possible to imagine how this place of worship and contemplation must have looked before it was destroyed at the behest of Henry VIII. A profoundly atmospheric place, Tintern inspired both JMW Turner and William Wordsworth. Today, it is the location of occasional son-et-lumiere performances and an annual candlelit carol service.

• Five miles north of Chepstow on the A466. www.cadw.wales.gov.uk

Tintern Parva. The little village next to the abbey extends along the bank of the Wye and is the focal point of numerous well-signed footpaths. The **Abbey Mill,** a water mill once operated by the monks, houses an arts and crafts centre, a gift shop and a café. **The Old Station** just up the valley is a preserved Victorian country

railway station with a signal box, and is a great spot for a picnic.
• Just north of the abbey; the village has grown along the river bank.
www.tintern.org.uk

....

Trellech

Ancient standing stones, known in English as Harold's Stones, give their name to this village: in Welsh, tre-llech means three stones or slates. In medieval times, this was a substantial town and the area has many sites of historic interest. Terret Tump is a forty-foot (12m) high mound of earth that was once the motte for one of the many small wooden castles built hurriedly by the Normans. Trellech's holy well –

St Anne's Well, or the Virtuous Well – used to be a place of pilgrimage. The churchyard contains a large pedestal, once the foundation for an ancient cross.
• Take the B4293 northward from Chepstow or southward from Monmouth.
www.wyenot.com/trellech.htm

Above left: **Tredegar House.** This symmetrical gem of restoration architecture is attractively set in fine parkland. Above right: **Tintern Abbey.** Located in an official Area of Outstanding Natural Beauty, the abbey has attracted tourists since Victorian times.

Usk

Usk Rural Life Museum.
Crammed with reminders of the region's rural heritage, this museum occupies the old **Malt Barn** in the attractive town of Usk. Follow the countryman's year as you see local wagons, vintage machinery and reconstructions of a farmhouse kitchen, laundry and dairy – and much more.
• The small town of Usk is just off the A449 north of Newport. Phone: 01291 673777

Wye Valley

Churches. Ancient churches abound in Monmouthshire, many of them in remote places. **St Martin's Church** at Cwmyoy stands on land that has subsided and no parts of its walls and tower seem to be square with any other. **Patrishow Church** is distinguished by a remarkable

Above: **Cwmyoy Church.** The walls and tower of Cwmyoy's remarkable church really do lean more than seems possible.
Right: **Wye Valley.** This Area of Outstanding Natural Beauty is a protected landscape surrounding a 72-mile stretch of the meandering river Wye between Chepstow and Hereford, along the border between England and Wales.

rood screen and loft dating from around 1500, a font bearing an inscription from around 1055, and a series of wall paintings. **Penallt Old Church** commands glorious views of the Wye valley.

• Cwmyoy and Patrishow are off the A465 north of Abergavenny; Penallt is just south of Monmouth, off the A466 or B4293.

Festivals and events

Abergavenny Food Festival. The liveliest, most cultured and quirkiest food festival in the UK, the Abergavenny Food Festival is held every **September** and celebrates the best of Welsh and British food. A must-visit for any food lover, the festival is held at numerous venues and streets in the town. Activities include cheese and wine tasting, chef's demos, and talks, as well as food stalls galore and a full programme of events.

• Phone: 01873 851643 www.abergavennyfoodfestival.com

Cultural festivals. For ten days each summer, the **Abergavenny Festival** brings a wide range of musical, dramatic, literary and visually artistic activity to the picturesque town. The **Tredegar House Folk Festival**, held every

Above and right: **Abergavenny Food Festival.** High-quality Welsh ingredients are celebrated, cooked, eaten and sold at the Abergavenny Food Festival.

May, sees dancers and musicians performing in traditional styles. The **Monmouth Festival** brings a wide choice of performances and exhibitions to the town during early August.

Llantilio Crossenny Festival of Music and Drama. This small village between Abergavenny and Monmouth is home to a high quality festival of classical music, opera and ballet, which has been held at **St Teilo's Church** each **May** for more than forty years.
• Mid-way between Abergavenny and Monmouth, on the B4233. Phone: 01873 856928
www.llantiliocrossenny.com

History brought to life.
The castles and historic houses of this south-eastern corner of Wales provide authentic locations for battle re-enactments and more gentle historically themed entertainments. Look out for military spectaculars, medieval days, son-et-lumiere displays, concerts and open-air theatre performances at the likes of **Caldicot**, **Usk**, **Abergavenny** and **Chepstow Castles** and the **Caerleon Roman amphitheatre**.
• Tourist Information Centres have dates and details of historical re-enactments.

Left: **Living history.** Look out for authentic re-enactments at castles and historic houses.
Above: **Abergavenny Food Festival.**

Where to eat and stay

Alphabetical listing with contact details of restaurants and accommodation

Angel Hotel*, Abergavenny
Phone: 01873 857121

Armless Dragon, Cardiff
Phone: 029 2038 2357
www.armlessdragon.co.uk

Bell at Skenfrith*, Skenfrith
Phone: 01600 750235
www.skenfrith.com

Chandlery Restaurant, Newport
Phone: 01633 256622

Clytha Arms*, Nr Abergavenny
Phone: 01873 840206
www.clytha-arms.com

Coed-y-Mwstwr, Bridgend
Phone: 01656 860621
www.coed-y-mwstwr.com

Da Venditto, Cardiff
Phone: 029 2023 0781
www.vendittogroup.co.uk/
davenditto.htm

Egerton Grey*, Barry
Phone: 01446 711666
www.egertongrey.co.uk

Felin Fach Griffin*, Felin Fach
Phone: 01874 620111
www.eatdrinksleep.ltd.uk

Foxhunter, Nant-y-Derry
Phone: 01873 881101
www.thefoxhunter.com

Frolics, Southerndown
Phone: 01656 880127

Great House*, Bridgend
Phone: 01656 657644
www.great-house-laleston.co.uk

Huddarts, Cowbridge
Phone: 01446 774645

La Marina, Penarth
Phone: 029 2070 5544

Le Gallois – Y Cymro, Cardiff
Phone: 029 2034 1264
www.legallois-ycymro.com

Old Post Office*, Cardiff
Phone: 029 2056 5400
www.old-post-office.com

Owens*, Newport
Phone: 01633 410262
www.celtic-manor.com

The Crown*, Whitebrook
Phone: 01600 860254
www.crownatwhitebrook.co.uk

The Hardwick, Abergavenny
Phone: 01873 854220

The Newbridge*, Tredunnock
Phone: 01633 451000
www.thenewbridge.co.uk

Walnut Tree, Nr Abergavenny
Phone: 01873 852797
www.thewalnuttreeinn.com

Woods Brasserie, Cardiff
Phone: 029 2049 2400
www.woods-brasserie.com

* Accommodation available

Information and useful websites

Tourist Information Centres throughout Wales have expert and welcoming staff who can offer independent assistance with planning routes, booking accommodation and the search for information on places or events to visit. They are your one-stop shop for holiday and short-break information, late availability and last-minute offers.

For a full list of Tourist Information Centres www.visitwales.com

Tourist Information Centres:
South WalesValleys
T 029 2022 7281

Cardiff and Glamorgan Vale
T 08701 211 258

Wye Valley and Vale of Usk
T 01291 623772

Useful websites

Castles and heritage:
www.cadw.wales.gov.uk
www.nationaltrust.org.uk
www.bbc.co.uk/wales/history

Museums and galleries:
www.museumwales.ac.uk
www.cymal.wales.gov.uk
(national and local museums)
www.artswales.org
www.artwales.com
www.chapter.org
www.thegate.org.uk
www.washingtongallery.co.uk

Festivals and events:
www.eisteddfod.org.uk
(the National Eisteddfod of Wales)
www.urdd.org (Urdd Youth Eisteddfod)
www.cardiffmusicals.com
(Festival of Musical Theatre)
www.thingstodo.org.uk
www.homecomingwales.com
www.cardiff-festival.com
www.millenniumstadium.com
www.wmc.org.uk
(Wales Millennium Centre)
www.wno.org.uk
(Welsh National Opera)
www.newtheatrecardiff.co.uk
www.stdavidshallcardiff.co.uk
www.shermantheatre.co.uk

Other websites
www.city-sightseeing.com
(Cardiff bus tours)
www.ccw.gov.uk (National Trails)
www.nationalparks.gov.uk
www.visitwales.com
www.wales.gov.uk
www.cardiff.gov.uk
www.newport.gov.uk

How to get here

By car. The UK's road network serves visitors to Wales well, making it easy to get to by car. You can get to south-east Wales along the M4.

By train. Wales is easy to get to from all of the UK. From London Paddington there is a frequent express service that will take you to Cardiff in only two hours.

If you are visiting from overseas you will find that there are good links between all major airports and the main rail network. For rail enquiries and booking ring + 44(0) 8457 48 49 50 or visit one of the following websites: www.nationalrail.co.uk, www.thetrainline.com or www.qjump.co.uk

By coach or bus. National Express offers a nationwide service of fast, reliable express coaches. There is a good service from London Victoria coach station to many towns and cities in Wales as well as from many cities and towns in both England and Scotland. For example, the journey time between London and Newport is around three hours. There are also convenient Flightlink coach services from major airports to destinations in Wales. For information and bookings call
+ 44 (0) 8705 808080 or go to:
www.nationalexpress.co.uk
Inside Wales there is an extensive network of regional and local bus services.

By air. There are regular direct flights to Cardiff International Airport from a wide range of destinations, including Amsterdam, Cork, Glasgow, London City, Paris and Prague. Also, Amsterdam, Dublin and Paris act as gateway hubs for European and international flights. For flight information call
+44 (0) 1446 711111
email infodesk@cwl.aero or visit
www.cial.co.uk
London's airports and those at Birmingham and Manchester are all good gateways to Wales. Each has good road and rail connections.

By sea. Three ferry companies operate services between south west Wales and Ireland. They are:
Irish Ferries.
Rosslare to Pembroke.
Tel: +44 (0) 8705 171717
www.irishferries.com
Stena Line. Rosslare to Fishgard.
Tel: +44 (0) 8705 707070
www.stenaline.co.uk
Swansea-Cork ferries.
Cork to Swansea.
Tel: +44 (0) 1792 456116
www.swanseacorkferries.com

Then travel along the M4 East to get to your destination.

Other ferry ports (along England's south coast and elsewhere) have good cross-country motorway and main road links to Wales.
   For car travellers arriving on the EuroTunnel service it is motorway all the way from Dover to Wales.

Castles and heritage throughout Wales

Most of the many archaeological sites, castles and historic houses of Wales, and numerous former centres of industry, are in the care of one of two agencies – Cadw or the National Trust. It is said that if a historic property has a roof, then it is likely to be run by the National Trust; otherwise it is probably the responsibility of Cadw. Not an infallible guide, of course, but a helpful start.

Wales has more castles and fortifications for its area than anywhere else in Europe.

Wales has more castles and fortifications for its area than anywhere else in Europe. If you include every earthwork revealed by archaeological surveys and aerial photography, there are more than six hundred sites. Their number and variety reflect the nation's turbulent and fascinating history.

In prehistoric times, life was a constant struggle for survival against the elements and attack by others. The earliest inhabitants of Wales made stone tools and weapons, but their limited building abilities were mainly directed at ceremonial matters and the commemoration of their dead. Though primitive fortifications exist, they are not substantial.

The **Celtic tribes**, who lived throughout what we now call the UK and Ireland before the arrival of the **Romans**, were notoriously warlike. The landscape – especially coastal promontories and hilltops with good views – is peppered with the remains of their substantial forts.

Above: **Chirk Castle.** The last of the castles built by Edward I in his conquest of Wales, Chirk Castle has fantastic gardens and a stunning view over nine counties.

The Romans introduced a sophisticated network of forts, barracks, roads and ports to sustain their legions as they encountered the troublesome tribes of the region they called **Cambria**. Many indigenous **Celts** eventually saw the advantage of adopting Roman ways, and their pragmatic co-operation made possible the governance of this remote extremity of the empire.

When the Romans began pulling out of their distant province of Britannia towards the end of the 4th century, the power vacuum was filled by regional rulers who provided the inspiration for the legendary **King Arthur**, mentioned for the first time in an early Welsh poem and later idealised into a paragon of chivalry.

The Saxons conquered much of what is now England but found Wales and Scotland fiercely resistant. During the 8th century, the eponymous **King Offa of Mercia** ordered the building of his dyke, a low earthwork that marked the western limit of his ambition and recognised the separateness of Wales.

On the Welsh side of **Offa's Dyke**, regional kings and princes consolidated their rule. Their courts were usually peripatetic and their households – families, soldiers, servants, minstrels and poets – moved between several castles. Through war, treaty and marriage their territories began to coalesce into an emerging Welsh nation.

In 1039, **Gruffudd ap Llywelyn** became the first ruler of a united and independent Welsh nation that was organised upon a sophisticated legal and constitutional foundation. But this was not the best timing. Within a couple of decades of the arrival of **William the Conqueror** in 1066, the **Normans** had taken the lands and powers of the Welsh princes in much of south-eastern Wales and were extending their influence and building their solid castles throughout the lowlands.

In 1267, **Llywelyn ap Gruffudd** was recognised by **Henry III as Prince of Wales**, but this harmonious arrangement was also short-lived. The English king **Edward I**, who came to power in 1272, aimed to bring Wales and Scotland fully under his rule. He spent vast sums in building his 'iron ring' of castles around Gwynedd, from where Llywelyn mounted his campaigns to retain

Clockwise from top left:
Gwydir Castle interior and exterior. Regarded as the finest Tudor house in Wales, Gwydir Castle was once the home to Katheryn of Berain, cousin of Elizabeth I.
Caldey Abbey. Caldey has been home to various orders of monks since Celtic times. Today the picturesque monastery overlooks the pretty island cottages, Village Green and Shop.
Tenby Tudor Merchant's House. This late 15th century town house is furnished to recreate the atmosphere of family life in Tudor times.

independence. Having succeeded in securing solid support throughout Wales against overwhelming forces, Llywelyn was eventually ambushed and killed at Cilmeri near Builth Wells in 1282.

Numerous fortified mansions and grand homes in the style of medieval castles have been built in Wales since those distant days of strife, but the pinnacle of castle building for military purposes was in the time of Edward I. The remarkable architecture and ingenuity of four of his castles – **Caernarfon, Conwy, Harlech** and **Beaumaris** – built by Master James of St George, the French genius in such matters, has been recognised in their collective designation as a UNESCO World Heritage Site.

Until the mid-18th century, Wales was a largely rural nation where landowners enjoyed the resources to build fine houses, and agricultural workers and their families lived modestly. The coastline was dotted with small harbours where fishing was the main activity.

The largest structures were the castles, which had long since outlived their purpose, and the great religious buildings, including the ruins of medieval abbeys.

The Industrial Revolution rapidly transformed the working pattern, the economy, the built environment and the social fabric of Wales. Within a few decades,

small towns and villages were transformed into some of the largest concentrations of industry in the world.

Merthyr Tydfil became the world's largest iron-producing centre, making possible the building of the railways. A pall of noxious fumes over **Swansea** and **Llanelli** reflected their specialisation in the smelting of copper, tin and other metals. Large numbers of people flocked to Wales from England and further afield, to provide manpower for the new industries.

The mining of coal in the south Wales Valleys boomed to the point where, by the early 20th century, 250,000 men toiled underground and **Cardiff** became the world's largest coal-exporting port. By this time, the combined population of the mining towns of the south Wales Valleys was equivalent – in number and variety of origin – to that of an additional large city.

Previous page: **Conwy Castle.** The castle's well-preserved walls give visitors the opportunity to walk along the top portions of the castle towers and town walls.
Above left: **Caerphilly Castle.** The castle was a revolutionary masterpiece of 13th century military planning due to its immense size (1.2h) and its large-scale use of water for defence.
Above right: **Menai Bridge.** At the time it was completed, Thomas Telford's bridge was the largest suspension bridge in the world.

The slate quarries of north and mid Wales expanded to meet the demand for roofing material at home, in Europe and in north America. Seaports grew to handle the thriving trade in raw materials and goods – and, as the railway network grew, to serve the passenger traffic to and from Ireland. Manufacturing industry expanded, particularly in south-eastern and north-eastern Wales.

Many of the industrial buildings and structures that made this ferment of activity possible – along with the grand houses built on its wealth – may be visited today. These heritage sites provide a fascinating insight into the way the people of Wales lived and worked in times gone by.

Several sites of the National Museum Wales (please see overleaf) provide especially direct insights into the industries that were so significant in shaping the appearance of the land and the character of the people.

Above: **Basingwerk Abbey.** During the 13th century Anglo-Welsh wars, Basingwerk's sympathies lay with the English. It apparently suffered little, and by the later 15th century had become quite prosperous. It was dissolved in 1536.
Left: **Bodnant Garden.** Spanning some 80 acres, Bodnant Garden is one of the most beautiful gardens in the UK.

Museums and galleries throughout Wales

In addition to the National Museums, you will find that most towns have a museum or heritage centre dedicated to the extraordinary variety of life and culture to be found in this deeply fascinating part of the world.

As befits a nation with such a rich history and well-preserved material heritage, Wales has many excellent museums.

As befits a nation with such a rich history and well-preserved material heritage, Wales has many excellent museums.

The **National Museum Wales** is a widely dispersed group of leading institutions. The **National Slate Museum** in Llanberis, tells how the quarrymen extracted the versatile building and roofing material from the mountains, and describes their tough lives. The

National Wool Museum in the Teifi valley is the place to try carding and spinning for yourself, and to learn all about wool production and use.

Few museums offer anything quite as dramatic as the underground tour at the **Big Pit National Coal Museum** near Blaenavon. And few put information technology to such

Above left: **Oriel Mostyn Gallery.** The Oriel Mostyn Gallery in Llandudno north Wales is one the UK's premier contemporary, modern and fine art galleries. Above right: **National Museum Cardiff.** The National Museum Cardiff houses one of Europe's finest art collections as well as preserving some of the nation's treasures.

effective use as the **National Waterfront Museum** in Swansea, which tells the story of the people of Wales at work, in industries old and new.

St Fagans National History Museum is one of Europe's very best open-air museums, featuring a wonderful collection of buildings relocated from all over Wales, together with absorbing indoor exhibitions about rural life and folk traditions.

The **National Museum Cardiff** is the nation's storehouse of all that is best in many and varied fields of interest – from archaeology to zoology, decorative arts, fine art, geology, science, technology and many other areas.

In addition to the National Museums, you will find that most towns have a museum or heritage centre dedicated to the extraordinary variety of life and culture to be found in this deeply fascinating part of the world.

Interesting museums include the **Llangollen Motor Museum** and **Pendine Museum of Speed**, the **National Coracle Centre**, which displays coracles from all over the world, the **Rhondda Heritage Park** and the **Blaenavon World Heritage Museum**, a testimony to the pre-eminence of south Wales as the world's major producer of iron and coal in the 19th century.

Wales has a long tradition of artistic expression, which continues today. Many gifted

artists and craftspersons live and work here and their work is sold from galleries and studios across the land. Collections of fine art, from Wales and elsewhere, have been assembled both by the nation and by individual collectors.

Collections of fine art, from Wales and elsewhere, have been assembled both by the nation and by individual collectors.

National Museum Cardiff displays many treasures including a significant collection of Impressionist works by Renoir, Monet and Cézanne. Eminent Welsh artists also feature, including 18th century landscape pioneers Richard Wilson and Thomas Jones, and 20th century artists Augustus John, Gwen John and Ceri Richards.

The **National Portrait Gallery** in Wales has over 100 portraits from the 19th century collections including works by John Singer Sargent and the Pre-Raphaelites.

The **Turner House Gallery** in Penarth shows fine art of the highest quality.

Above: **National Portrait Gallery.** The National Portrait Gallery at Bodelwyddan Castle houses many wonderful portraits from the 19th century.

Artist's palette

The westernmost regions of Wales (especially Anglesey, Snowdonia and Pembrokeshire) have inspired many artists. Look out for pleasing depictions of landscape, seascape, the seasons and rural life by Sir Kyffin Williams RA, William Selwyn, Rob Piercy, John Knapp-Fisher, Donald McIntyre and others.

Clusters of high-quality artists' studios may be found at Glynllifon (near Caernarfon), Ruthin, Hay-on-Wye and St Clears.

The biennial **Artes Mundi** competition at the **National Museum Cardiff** features the work of international conceptual artists.

Above left: **St Fagans.**
St Fagans Castle with its splendid Rose Garden is only one of many buildings you can explore in this informative open-air museum. Step back in time as far as the Iron Age and experience how Welsh people once lived and worked.

Above right: **National Waterfront Museum.** At the National Museum Wales's newest attraction you can experience noise, grime, high finance, upheaval, consumerism and opportunity and see how Wales's Industrial Revolution help shape the rest of the world.

Left: **Aberystwyth Arts Centre.**
The award-winning Aberystwyth Arts Centre has a wide-ranging programme of events and activities across all art forms. It is recognised as a national centre for arts development and welcomes over 650,000 visitors a year through their doors.

Festivals and events throughout Wales

There are festivals in Wales for just about every aspect of culture. You will find everything from large national events to local musical and literary festivals, carnivals, regattas and shows that draw the crowds to historic villages, towns and harbours.

You will find everything from large national events to local musical and literary festivals, carnivals, regattas and shows that draw the crowds to historic villages, towns and harbours.

The main tourism season in Wales extends from Easter onwards, through the summer, until the school term begins in early September. Countless events, suitable for all the family, are organised during these months. Many places also provide ample reason to visit throughout the year, by organising activities and entertainment appropriate to autumn, Christmas, and other times.

Above left: **Aberystwyth and Ceredigion County Show.** This County Show is one of many across Wales that promote agriculture and bring together the farming industry and the local community. Shows like these hold a number of events that make great days out for visitors.
Above right: **The Big Cheese, Caerphilly.** This is an annual celebration of local and Welsh heritage, history, culture and entertainment. The festival includes jugglers, fire eaters, living history re-enactments, music, funfair rides and more.

Musical, literary and theatrical enthusiasms feature strongly and you will find performances at every level from professional venue to village hall. The orchestra of **Welsh National Opera** and the **BBC National Orchestra of Wales** appear at spectacular open-air concerts each summer; at Swansea's Proms in the Park, Cardiff Bay and elsewhere.

Musical styles ranging from classical to brass bands, and from jazz to folk and roots music, have strong followings at festivals, halls and clubs across the land. Authentic Welsh folk traditions, including music and dance, are still celebrated, notably in and around Cardiff, at the beginning of May and at Christmas and New Year.

The traditions of the countryside are a recurrent theme, central to the identity of many Welsh people. Despite the demands of the farming life, the seasonal pattern allows time for the agricultural shows at local and national level. The largest of these, the **Royal Welsh Agricultural Show** is held at Builth Wells during **July**, with the **Winter Fair** following at the same venue early in **December**. Smaller shows, to which all are welcome, are organised at county level throughout Wales.

Some of the more vigorous, and occasionally dangerous, traditional sports have disappeared but Wales has made a unique contribution in this area

of endeavour. The little town of **Llanwrtyd Wells** has become famous for its calendar of what can only be described as profoundly wacky challenges, including the **world bog- snorkelling championships**! The latter requires an unusual ability to ignore the cold and unsavoury surroundings, and to navigate in zero visibility, as you swim as rapidly as you can for the finish line.

The largest annual events arrive one after the other during the spring, summer and early autumn. Typically organised by experienced professionals supported by resourceful local committees, they feature big names in their respective fields and provide a visitor experience second-to-none.

Llanwrtyd Wells has become famous for its world bog- snorkelling championships!

Above: **Welsh National Opera at Cardiff Bay.** The Oval Basin at Cardiff Bay hosts fabulous open-air concerts by big names, including Welsh National Opera, as well as being a venue for other events such as Cardiff's International Food and Drink Festival.

The Hay Festival of Literature, held each May, sees world-famous authors, and enthusiastic readers.

The **Hay Festival of Literature**, held each **May**, sees world-famous authors, and enthusiastic readers who appreciate a good book, congregating at the small town of Hay-on-Wye, which has more than 30 bookshops.

Brecon pulsates to the sounds of jazz during **August**, when traditional bands and skilled solo practitioners of the more rarified forms come to town for the **Brecon Jazz Festival**.

Bryn Terfel, the world's leading bass-baritone, invites world-class guests to join him on stage before an enthusiastic home audience at his annual **Faenol Festival** (voted Best Show in Wales) held near Bangor each **August** Bank Holiday.

The Cardiff Festival offers an exciting series of concerts throughout the summer.

The **Cardiff Festival** offers an exciting series of concerts, a multicultural carnival, a harbour festival, food shows, sports competitions and many other events throughout the summer, in the city centre and at Cardiff Bay.

Celebrations of food and produce, including the **Abergavenny Food Festival**, make a point of inviting local companies to provide the best possible food and drink – both home-produced and more exotic.

The largest of Wales's cultural festivals – in fact, one of the largest in Europe, with a daily attendance typically exceeding 20,000 – is the **National Eisteddfod**. This week-long gathering follows a tradition established by Lord Rhys at Cardigan Castle in 1176, whereby poets and musicians (and nowadays many other talented and creative participants) meet in a spirit of friendly competition.

Clockwise from top left:
Hay Literature Festival. This world-renowned literary festival hosts talks and book signings of the biggest names of the time. Authors from around the world come here to promote their new books. A must for book-lovers.
Brecon Jazz Festival. One of the best jazz festivals in Europe and all the tickets to see the big names performing will go fast. Even if you don't have a ticket, you can soak up the Festival's vibrant atmosphere.
Abergavenny Food Festival. Eagerly awaited by foodies, the Abergavenny Food Festival is one of the largest in the UK.

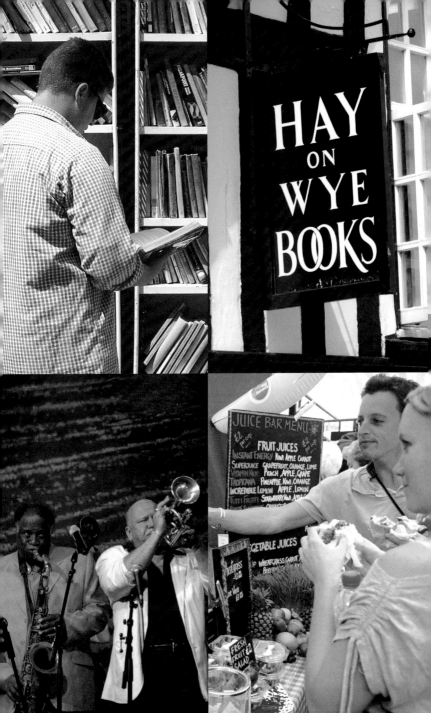

The largest of Wales's cultural festivals – in fact, one of the largest in Europe, with a daily attendance typically exceeding 20,000 – is the National Eisteddfod.

Held at the beginning of **August**, the **National Eisteddfod** moves to a different part of Wales each year. The enormous pavilion, venue for competitions and evening concerts, seats some 3,500 people. The surrounding Maes, or campus, has several smaller performance and exhibition spaces and upwards of 300 stands, where most of Wales's cultural and educational organisations are represented.

The central point of the **National Eisteddfod** is that everything happens in the Welsh language. Simultaneous-translation receivers are available at the main entrance and anyone wishing to learn the language will be made welcome at the Learners' Pavilion – there's a hotly contested prize for Welsh Learner of the Year.

The principle of friendly competition has been extended worldwide by the **Llangollen International Musical Eisteddfod**. This captivating multicultural gathering originated in 1947 as a means of bringing together like-

minded people from all over war-ravaged Europe. One of its most moving moments being the first appearance by a choir from Germany in 1949. Performers of appropriately high ability nowadays travel from all over the world to attend in a spirit of shared appreciation.

Little wonder then, that this is the only festival in the world to have been nominated for the Nobel Peace Prize.

Performers of appropriately high ability nowadays travel from all over the world to attend in a spirit of shared appreciation.

Above left: **Royal Welsh Show.** The Royal Welsh Show is one of the most prestigious events of its type in Europe, and brings to together the farming industry and rural community in a celebration of the best of British agriculture with a unique and very special 'Welsh' flavour.

Above right: **Cardiff Festival.** Cardiff Festival is the UK's largest free outdoor festival, and brings colour and cultural vibrancy to the city and the waterfront area of Cardiff Bay.

The Welsh language

The ancient language of Wales is very much alive during the 21st century and is spoken by around half a million people.

Welsh evolved from the Celtic languages spoken throughout Britain at the time of the Roman occupation. These included two distinct forms: the Goidelic group, which produced the Irish, Scots Gaelic and Manx (Isle of Man) languages, and the Brythonic group, from which the Welsh, Cornish and Breton languages emerged.

Welsh is one of Europe's oldest languages and is by far the strongest survivor of all the Celtic tongues. As with all languages, it has over many centuries absorbed words and influences from elsewhere.

There is no compulsion to speak Welsh but many people deeply enjoy doing so. The lyrical nature of the language seems designed to produce pleasingly poetic sounds and opens the door to a treasure trove of culture. Even the smallest attempt at learning the basics will be much appreciated by the people you meet, even if they need to help you a little with some of the pronunciation.

The language is generally phonetic, so that each letter represents only one sound: what is written is what you say. Some of the sounds however differ from English, as follows:

'a' as in 'apple'
'e' as in 'exit'
'i' as in 'ee'
'o' as in office
'u' sounds similar to the 'i' in 'win', but longer
'w' as in 'win' - serves as a vowel
'y' as the 'u' in 'cup', but longer – serves as a vowel
the famous 'll' is akin to the 'tl' sound in the English words 'antler' or 'Bentley'- but you breathe out gently as you say it.
the Welsh 'ch' is similar to that in Johann Sebastian Bach, a highly regarded figure in Wales!
'dd' sounds like the 'th' in then
'th' sounds like the 'th' in thing

Websites

www.bwrdd-yr-iaith.org.uk (information on the Welsh language)
www.bbc.co.uk/wales/learnwelsh

A few helpful words and phrases

Good morning	Bore da
Good afternoon	Prynhawn da
Goodbye	Hwyl fawr
Good evening	Noswaith dda
Good health!/Cheers	Iechyd da!
Good night	Nos da
How are you?	Sut mae?
Very good	Da iawn
Welcome	Croeso
Welcome to Wales	Croeso i Gymru
fine thanks	iawn diolch
yes	ie
no	na
please	os gwelwch yn dda
Thank you	Diolch
Good	Da
small	bach
big	mawr
where is?	ble mae?
castle	castell
river	afon
food	bwyd
drink	diod
I'd like a pint of...	Hoffwn i beint o...
And a glass of...	a gwydriad o...
Where am I?	Ble ydw i?
I'm lost!	Dwi ar goll!
Where's the nearest cashpoint?	Ble mae'r twll yn y wal agosaf?

Graffeg books

Graffeg publish illustrated books about contemporary life in Wales. Each book is focused on a particular interest: landscapes, food, lifestyle, heritage, architecture, festivals, music, arts, sports and culture. Graffeg books make wonderful guides, travelling companions and gifts.

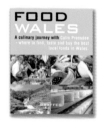

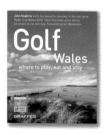

View our catalogue online www.graffeg.com

Visit our website for the latest news and view the Graffeg book list online @ ww.graffeg.com Browse through books online before you order.

Published by Graffeg.
Tel: 029 2037 7312
sales@graffeg.com
www.graffeg.com

About the authors

Written by
David Williams

David Williams is a writer and photographer having a wide-ranging knowledge of the life, culture and history of Wales. He wrote, and supplied images

for, the Graffeg books Landscape Wales, About Cardiff and About Wales – and for other titles in this series of pocket guides. He works for numerous book and magazine publishers, broadcasters, tourism authorities and cultural organisations. A graduate of the University of Wales, he is a fluent Welsh speaker.

As a contributor to Photolibrary Wales, his images help to promote Wales worldwide. Having travelled throughout Wales, he is thoroughly familiar with its people and places, and able to offer a balanced perspective on the whole of our compact but enormously fascinating nation.

Foreword by
Siân Lloyd

Originally from Neath, Siân Lloyd attended school in Ystalyfera and studied at the universities of Cardiff and Oxford. She worked as a television presenter with

S4C, and as a radio and television journalist, before joining the ITV national weather team. She reports on the environment for ITN, and on travel and environmental matters for national newspapers.

Her wide spectrum of television appearances, as presenter and guest, includes children's programmes, quizzes, chat shows, talent shows, consumer programmes and current-affairs discussions. Her interests include food – cooking it, eating it, and writing and making programmes about it! – mountain walking (from Wales to the Alps), chess, Scrabble, films and theatre.

Index

A

Abbey Mill, The 62
Abergavenny 53
Abergavenny Castle 56
Abergavenny Festival 66
Abergavenny Food Festival 66
Abergavenny Museum 53
Albany Gallery 34

B

Barry 25
Barry Tall Ships Festival 51
Bay Art 36
Berwyn Centre 49
Big Balloon, The 22
Big Cheese, The 22
Big Pit National Coal Museum 15
Big Welsh Bite, The 23
Blaenavon 14
Blaenavon Community Heritage and Cordell Museum 17
Blaenavon UNESCO World Heritage Site 14
Blaengarw Workmens' Hall 49
Border castles 56
Brecon Beacons 18
Bridgend 25
Brinore Tramroad 17
Bryngarw House 26
Brynmawr 17
Brynmenyn 26
Butetown History and Arts Centre 27

C

Caerleon 53
Caerleon amphitheatre 53
Caerleon International Sculpture and Arts Festival 54
Caerleon's Roman Legionary Museum 54
Caerphilly 17
Caerphilly Castle 17
Caerwent 54
Caldicot Castle 56
Cardiff 26
Cardiff Bay 35
Cardiff Castle 29
Cardiff City Hall 26
Cardiff city venues 31
Cardiff Festival 49
Cardiff International Food and Drink Festival 50
Cardiff Singer of the World 33, 49
Castell Coch 48
Chapter Arts 33
Chepstow 55
Chepstow Castle 55, 56
Chepstow Museum 55
Cold Knap, Barry 25
Coliseum Theatre 13
Cosmeston Medieval Village 44
Cowbridge 42
Cyfarthfa Castle 18
Cyfarthfa Castle Museum and Art Gallery 18
Cynon Valley Museum 13

D

Dyffryn Gardens 47

E

Elliot Colliery winding house 19

F

Ffwrwm Art and Craft Centre 54
Fourteen Locks Canal Centre 60

G

Gŵyl Ifan 50
Goytre Wharf 57
Grosmont Castle 56

H

Heritage Weekend 51
History brought to life 69

I

International Festival of Musical Theatre 49

J

Jazz in the Park 23

K

Kooywood Gallery 34

Index